Read · Reason · Write

Threatened Species

by Jack Cassidy, Ph.D., Drew Cassidy, M.Ed., and Douglas J. Loveless

Credits

Cover and title page: www.istockphoto.com/alexmanig

Page 5: www.istockphoto.com/HelenEGrose; Page 12: Image used under Creative Commons from Fred Schwohl; Page 13: Image used under Creative Commons from Bart Swanson; Page 19: www.istockphoto.com/holgs; Page 20: www.shutterstock.com, Brandon Seidel; Page 39: Image used under Creative Commons from Kent Backman; Page 40: www.istockphoto.com/PictureLake; Page 46: Image used under Creative Commons from Manuel Heinrich; Page 47: Image used under Creative Commons from Mila Zinkova; Page 54: Image used under Creative Commons from Nick Hobgood; Page 61: Image used under Creative Commons from Terry Gross.

Copyright © 2010 The Continental Press, Inc.

No part of this publication may be reproduced in any form or by any means, electronic, mechanical, photocopying, recording, or otherwise, without the prior written permission of the publisher. All rights reserved. Printed in the United States of America.

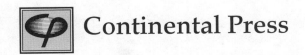

Continental Press

CONTENTS

What This Book Is About

In this book, you will read about animals that are threatened or endangered. This means that there aren't many of them left. Some of these animals are large. Some are not so large. Some of the animals live on the land. Others live in the water.

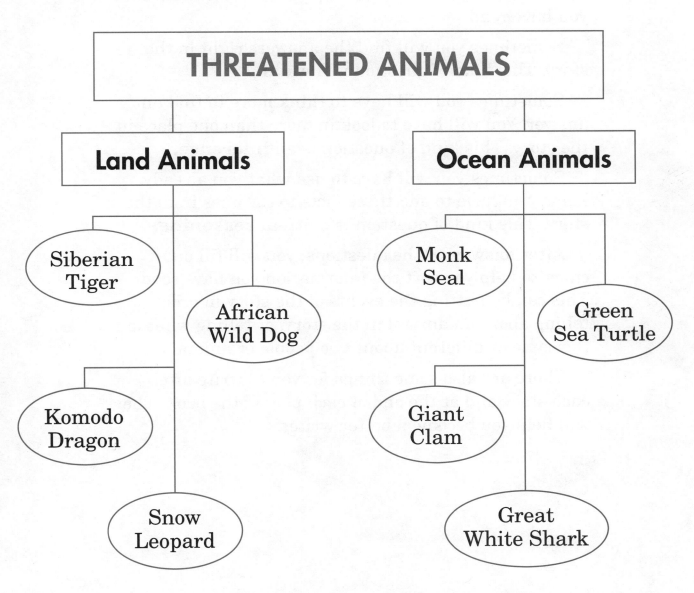

THREATENED ANIMALS

Land Animals

- Siberian Tiger
- African Wild Dog
- Komodo Dragon
- Snow Leopard

Ocean Animals

- Monk Seal
- Green Sea Turtle
- Giant Clam
- Great White Shark

Have fun reading this book about endangered animals!

© The Continental Press, Inc.   DUPLICATING THIS MATERIAL IS ILLEGAL.

How to Use This Book

After you read each story, you will see some questions. They will help you think about the story. There are also questions at the end of each part of the book. All the questions will help you understand what you have read.

Sometimes you will find the answers right in the story. This kind of question is **factual.**

Sometimes you will have to think more to find an answer. You will have to look in more than one place in the story. This kind of question is an **inference.**

Sometimes you will have to use what you already know. You have to add these facts to the ones from the story. This kind of question is **critical reasoning.**

After answering the questions, you will fill out a chart to help you sort the information you have read. This can be putting the events of the story in order, telling about an animal in the story, or telling what is the same or different about two people or animals.

There are also some things for you to write after each story and at the end of each part of the book. They will help you become a better writer.

© The Continental Press, Inc.   **DUPLICATING THIS MATERIAL IS ILLEGAL.**

The Biggest Cats

Do you know what the biggest cat is? This animal grows to be almost 11 feet long. It has a tail that can measure 3 feet. It can weigh up to 660 pounds. The animal's body is covered with striped fur.

Have you guessed what the animal is?

The biggest cat uses its camouflage to hide. This makes it easier to hunt. It sneaks up on prey and pounces.

Have you guessed yet?

The biggest cat lives alone. It marks its territory with its scent to keep its rivals away. This powerful cat travels many miles to hunt. It eats large animals like elk and wild boar. It can eat as much as 60 pounds in one night. It hunts by stealth at night, sneaking up on its prey.

© The Continental Press, Inc. **DUPLICATING THIS MATERIAL IS ILLEGAL.**

The biggest cat is the tiger. And the biggest tiger is the Siberian tiger.

What else do you know about Siberian tigers? Do you know that:

Female tigers raise their young with no help from the males

Cubs cannot hunt until they are 18 months old

Cubs live with their mothers for two or three years

A Siberian tiger's roar can be heard two miles away

They live in southeast Russia near China

The Siberian tiger is just one type of tiger. There were eight types of species. They were called *subspecies*. A subspecies is a type of species. Three of the types of tigers have now become extinct. They were all killed. One type was the Caspian tiger. The Bali tiger is extinct, too. Javan tigers are also gone. These three types do not exist any more.

Now the most common type of tiger is the Bengal tiger. These tigers live in India. They make up about half of all tigers. There are fewer Siberian tigers. Only 300 are left in the wild.

Every year, there are fewer Siberian tigers. Do you know why? They are losing their homes. People chop down the forests where the tigers live. The tigers have lost their *habitats*. Poachers also kill Siberian tigers. These people hunt the animals even though it is against the law. Some people hunt them for trophies. Siberian tigers are also used in some traditional medicines in Asia.

Today, people are trying to protect Siberian tigers. They have made special animal parks. These parks are called *reserves*. But more needs to be done to help these cats.

© The Continental Press, Inc. **DUPLICATING THIS MATERIAL IS ILLEGAL.**

Understanding the Story

It is important to understand what you read. You just read a story about Siberian tigers. Did you read the story carefully? Here are some questions about the story. Read each one. Then fill in the circle beside the best answer. If you are not sure, go back and look at the story again.

1. What is the main idea of this story?

   Ⓐ There are many big animals in Siberia.

   Ⓑ Poachers kill many endangered animals.

   Ⓒ Nobody knows which animal is the biggest.

   Ⓓ The biggest cat is the Siberian tiger.

   Inference

   D is the correct answer. The passage is mostly about the Siberian tiger so you can infer that D is the main idea.

2. What do you think happens when people cut down forests in places where Siberian tigers live?

   Ⓐ The Siberian tigers leave the people alone.

   Ⓑ The Siberian tigers lose their homes.

   Ⓒ The Siberian tigers eat the people.

   Ⓓ The people like having the Siberian tigers around.

   Critical Reasoning

   B is the correct answer. You must think critically and realize that when people cut down the places where Siberian tigers live, the tigers lose their homes.

© The Continental Press, Inc.   **DUPLICATING THIS MATERIAL IS ILLEGAL.**

3. Which is <u>not</u> true?

(A) Siberian tigers can pounce to hunt their food.

(B) Siberian tigers can be 11 feet long.

(C) Siberian tigers use camouflage to hunt.

(D) There are more Siberian tigers than any other type.

Inference

D is the correct answer. The Bengal tiger is the most common type of tiger so you can infer that there are more Bengal than Siberian tigers.

4. Why do some Siberian tigers now live in animal parks?

(A) They like it there.

(B) They have lost their other homes.

(C) There is no water there.

(D) There is more food there.

Inference

B is the correct answer. The parks were made to provide tigers with a home so you can infer that they live there because they lost their natural home.

5. Siberian tigers are killed

(A) for their meat   (C) because they are scary

(B) to be trophies   (D) for their territory

Factual

B is the correct answer. The passage says that tigers are killed to be trophies. This is a factual question.

© The Continental Press, Inc.   **DUPLICATING THIS MATERIAL IS ILLEGAL.**

6. Poachers are people who

(A) kill animals illegally

(B) protect animals

(C) chase animals away from farms

(D) feed animals

Inference

A is the correct answer. The passage says that poachers kill tigers even though it is against the law so you can infer that poachers are people who kill animals illegally.

7. How many subspecies of tigers have become extinct?

(A) 3   (C) 6

(B) 5   (D) 8

Factual

A is the correct answer. The passage says that three species have become extinct. This is a factual question.

8. Why are Siberian tigers at greater risk for extinction than Bengal tigers?

(A) Siberian tigers are meaner.

(B) Siberian tigers are easier to hunt.

(C) There are more Siberian tigers.

(D) There are fewer Siberian tigers.

Critical Reasoning

D is the correct answer. The passage says that Bengal tigers are the most common so you can infer that there are fewer Siberian tigers.

© The Continental Press, Inc.   DUPLICATING THIS MATERIAL IS ILLEGAL.

Summing Up

This story gave you some information about Siberian tigers. It told you what they look like, what they like to do, and why they are endangered.

An **idea web** is a way to help you organize facts. The center circle tells you what the idea web is about. The outer circles tell you certain things about tigers. Fill in the circles with things you learned from the story. If you need help, go back and look at the story again. Some facts have already been filled in for you.

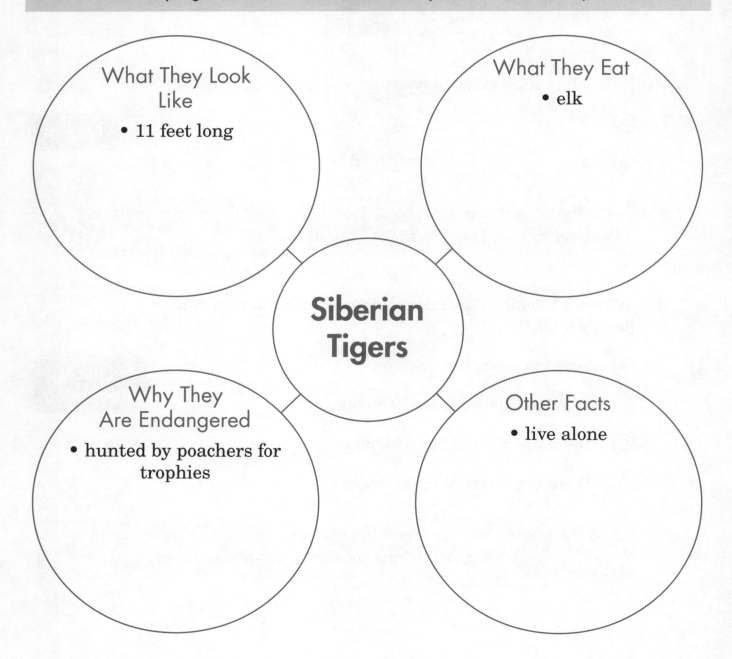

What They Look Like
- 11 feet long

What They Eat
- elk

Siberian Tigers

Why They Are Endangered
- hunted by poachers for trophies

Other Facts
- live alone

Read · Reason · Write ·

© The Continental Press, Inc.   **DUPLICATING THIS MATERIAL IS ILLEGAL.**

Write About It

Describing words help your reader get a good picture of what something looks like or about the actions that are taking place. These words often tell about size, shape, and color. They can also tell about feelings and actions. Imagine you are a visitor from another planet. Your ship has landed next to a Siberian tiger. You've never seen anything like this creature! Write a journal entry about the Siberian tiger. Describe what it looks like and what it does. Try to use describing words in your writing.

Date: _____

Today we landed on a new planet. We saw a strange animal. We believe

it is called a Siberian tiger. It looks like _____

_____

_____

_____

The tiger did interesting things. It _____

_____

_____

_____

I think this creature is _____

_____

_____

_____

© The Continental Press, Inc. **DUPLICATING THIS MATERIAL IS ILLEGAL.**

The Painted Dog

Dogs roam the grasslands of Africa. They look like they have been painted. The dogs are not anyone's pets. Though they look like a dog you might have as a pet, they are wild. They run free. They are called African wild dogs.

These dogs are also called painted dogs because of their coloring. These dogs have fur that looks like someone painted it. Their coats have patches of red, black, brown, white, and yellow fur. Each dog has a different painted coat just like each person has different fingerprints.

The African wild dogs are different from *domesticated* dogs. Domesticated dogs are dogs people keep as pets. Wild dogs can't be kept as pets. Also, the African wild dogs only have four toes on each foot. Other dogs have five toes.

© The Continental Press, Inc.   **DUPLICATING THIS MATERIAL IS ILLEGAL.**

African wild dogs are like wolves. They live in packs of 6 to 20 dogs. The packs used to be bigger. But there are fewer of these dogs now. The dogs in a pack share food and help sick members. The dogs cooperate and communicate by touch, action, and *vocalizations* like barking.

These dogs hunt together, too. They hunt antelopes and bigger animals, too. They also eat rodents and birds. When people live close, the wild dogs will eat cows, goats, and chickens.

Living near people has led to problems. First, farmers kill the dogs to keep their animals, or livestock, safe. Also, African wild dogs get sick from diseases. They get sick from diseases carried by domestic animals. There is also less land for them to roam. The dogs lose their homes as people move and settle the land. All of this has led to the African wild dog becoming endangered. Endangered animals could die out, and there would be no more of them. There are less that 4,000 wild dogs left.

© The Continental Press, Inc. **DUPLICATING THIS MATERIAL IS ILLEGAL.**

Understanding the Story

Here are some questions about the story. Read each one. Then fill in the circle beside the best answer. If you are not sure, go back and look at the story again.

1. African wild dogs

   Ⓐ   are just like a pet dog

   Ⓑ   have five toes

   Ⓒ   live alone

   Ⓓ   look painted

Inference

2. African wild dogs are endangered mainly because

   Ⓐ   they do not have many babies

   Ⓑ   they do not live very long

   Ⓒ   there are too many of them

   Ⓓ   farmers kill them to protect livestock

Critical Reasoning

3. Animals that are endangered

   Ⓐ   are very dangerous

   Ⓑ   could die out, and there would be no more of them

   Ⓒ   live in Africa and eat grass

   Ⓓ   are smaller than an African wild dog

Factual

© The Continental Press, Inc. **DUPLICATING THIS MATERIAL IS ILLEGAL.**

4. How are wolves and wild dogs alike?

(A) They both live in the snow.

(B) They like people.

(C) They are the same color.

(D) They live and hunt in packs.

Critical Reasoning

5. If you see an African wild dog, you should

(A) try to feed it

(B) keep it as a pet

(C) try to kill it

(D) leave it alone

Critical Reasoning

6. *Domesticated* dogs are

(A) nice dogs

(B) beautiful dogs

(C) dogs that can be pets

(D) dogs that live in the wild

Inference

© The Continental Press, Inc.   DUPLICATING THIS MATERIAL IS ILLEGAL.

7. *Vocalizations* are

    Ⓐ sounds that African wild dogs use to communicate

    Ⓑ sounds that people use to call their dogs

    Ⓒ meaningless sounds that African wild dogs make

    Ⓓ songs

Inference

8. African wild dogs eat

    Ⓐ antelope

    Ⓑ pigs

    Ⓒ snakes

    Ⓓ fish

Inference

© The Continental Press, Inc. **DUPLICATING THIS MATERIAL IS ILLEGAL.**

Summing Up

You have learned some things about African wild dogs. A **Venn diagram** is a special way to compare and contrast two things. Look at the Venn diagram below. Fill in the middle circle. Write how African wild dogs and domesticated dogs are the same. Fill in the other circles. Write how African wild dogs and domesticated dogs are different. Here are some words to help you:

size	four toes	five toes	lives in packs
fur	hunts	mean	peaceful
like a wolf	wild	lives with people	is hunted
kept as a pet	four legs	tame	fed their food

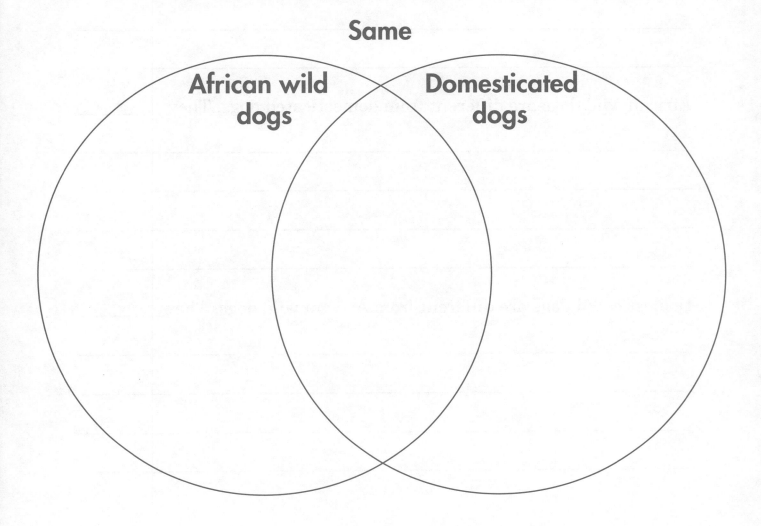

Same

African wild dogs

Domesticated dogs

© The Continental Press, Inc. **DUPLICATING THIS MATERIAL IS ILLEGAL.**

Write About It

When you **compare** things, you tell how they are alike. When you **contrast** things, you tell how they are different. You should also give facts to back up your ideas.

Write about how African wild dogs and domesticated dogs are the same. Then write about how African wild dogs and domesticated dogs are different. Use your Venn diagram to help you. The first sentence of each paragraph has been done for you.

African wild dogs and domesticated dogs are alike in some ways. For

example, they both _____

_____

_____

African wild dogs are different from domesticated dogs. They _____

_____

_____

_____

Domesticated dogs are different from African wild dogs. They _____

_____

_____

_____

© The Continental Press, Inc.   DUPLICATING THIS MATERIAL IS ILLEGAL.

Dinosaur or Dragon?

You are on a small island in Indonesia. You find a tree to hide behind. You see a small deer eating grass. Suddenly a huge animal runs at the deer. Its long tail whips around. It soon kills the deer and begins to eat it.

What is this huge monster? It looks like a dinosaur, but it isn't. And it isn't a dragon, either. It is the world's largest lizard, the Komodo dragon.

This lizard can be 10 feet long and weigh 200 pounds. It has more than 50 razor-sharp teeth, and its saliva is poisonous. A Komodo dragon can kill a deer or a pig. If it finds a dead animal, it will eat that, too. It can smell dead animals from far away. It sticks its forked tongue in and out to test the air for signs of food.

© The Continental Press, Inc.   DUPLICATING THIS MATERIAL IS ILLEGAL.

Like all lizards, Komodo dragons are reptiles. They are cold-blooded animals. When reptiles get too cold, they have to lie in the sun to warm up. When they get too hot, they hide in the shade. Sometimes they go into a water hole to cool down. Reptiles lay eggs. The mother Komodo dragon digs a hole in the ground to lay her eggs. She lays about 28 at a time.

Komodo dragons are rare. There are only a few thousand of them in the world. They live on only a few islands in Indonesia. One of these is Komodo. The island gave the dragon its name.

Komodo dragons are endangered. People hunt deer and pigs, just like the large lizards do. Then the Komodo dragons don't have enough to eat. Poachers kill the Komodo dragons, too. And farmers push the lizards off the land. That is why Komodo dragons are "protected." In Komodo National Park, many people come just to see the dragons. People who live there raise goats to feed the large lizards. They want to make sure that we always have "dragons" on Earth.

© The Continental Press, Inc.   **DUPLICATING THIS MATERIAL IS ILLEGAL.**

Here are some questions about the story that you just read. Read each one. Then fill in the circle beside the best answer. If you are not sure, go back and look at the story again.

1. The main idea of this story is that Komodo dragons

   Ⓐ eat deer

   Ⓑ are like crocodiles

   Ⓒ are the world's largest lizards

   Ⓓ live in Indonesia

   Inference

2. Another word for *saliva* is

   Ⓐ poison

   Ⓑ drool

   Ⓒ teeth

   Ⓓ tongue

   Critical Reasoning

3. Which is <u>true</u> about Komodo dragons?

   Ⓐ They weigh 200 pounds.

   Ⓑ They are warm-blooded animals.

   Ⓒ They are big, friendly lizards.

   Ⓓ They live in many places.

   Factual

© The Continental Press, Inc. **DUPLICATING THIS MATERIAL IS ILLEGAL.**

4. Komodo dragons eat

Inference

(A) only pigs and goats

(B) only deer and goats

(C) only animals that they kill

(D) almost any meat they can find

5. Why do you think people come to see the Komodo dragons?

Critical Reasoning

(A) They want to learn about these real-life "dragons."

(B) They want to bring one home for a pet.

(C) They get to choose one Komodo dragon to let loose in the wild.

(D) They want to learn how to hunt them.

6. The word *protected* in this story means that

Critical Reasoning

(A) Komodo dragons are kept in a zoo

(B) Komodo dragons are kept behind a fence on an island

(C) it is against the law to feed Komodo dragons

(D) it is against the law to kill Komodo dragons

© The Continental Press, Inc. **DUPLICATING THIS MATERIAL IS ILLEGAL.**

7. Komodo dragons use their tongues to

Factual

   (A) poison their food

   (B) smell for food

   (C) take care of their babies

   (D) clean themselves

8. People hunt deer and pigs. Why is this a problem for Komodo dragons?

Inference

   (A) Deer and pigs help raise young Komodo dragons.

   (B) Deer and pigs find food for the Komodo dragons to eat.

   (C) Deer and pigs dig holes for Komodo dragons to lay their eggs.

   (D) Deer and pigs are the Komodo dragons' food.

© The Continental Press, Inc. **DUPLICATING THIS MATERIAL IS ILLEGAL.**

Summing Up

You have learned some interesting facts about Komodo dragons. It often helps to sort new things we know so we can remember them.

Below is a **diagram** to help you sort information about Komodo dragons. The center of the diagram tells you what the diagram is about. Each part of the diagram tells something special about Komodo dragons. Fill in the rest of the diagram. Use the facts at the bottom of the page and information from the story. Be sure to put each one in the right place.

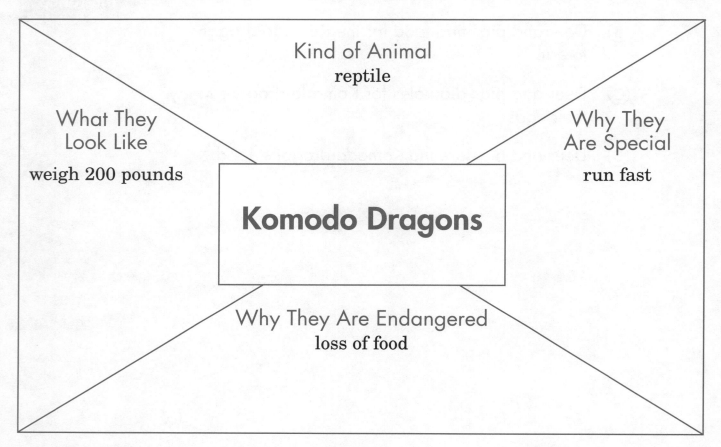

Kind of Animal
reptile

What They
Look Like

weigh 200 pounds

Why They
Are Special

run fast

Komodo Dragons

Why They Are Endangered

loss of food

cold-blooded	forked tongue	lay eggs
loss of habitat	10 feet long	only a few thousand
largest lizard	long, strong tail	poisonous saliva
smell for food	only on a few islands	poachers

© The Continental Press, Inc.   **DUPLICATING THIS MATERIAL IS ILLEGAL.**

Write About It

A good writer has to practice. You have to think about how to put words together. One way to do this is to list some important words about what you want to say. Then write a sentence using those words.

Here are some words that tell about Komodo dragons. Use the words to write interesting sentences about these animals. The first one is done for you. Use your diagram to help you do the rest.

1.   Komodo dragons   reptiles

The Komodo dragons are reptiles.
_____

2.   reptiles   cold-blooded   eggs

_____

3.   lizards   200 pounds   10 feet long

_____

4.   run fast   catch   deer and pigs

_____

5.   live   island   Indonesia

_____

6.   a few thousand   Komodo dragons   world

_____

7.   Komodo dragons   50 teeth   saliva

_____

© The Continental Press, Inc.   **DUPLICATING THIS MATERIAL IS ILLEGAL.**

This story is about an endangered animal living in the mountains of Asia. Read the story. Then answer the questions that follow.

Snow Leopards

Walking in the snow can be hard work. With each step, you sink deeper. People use snowshoes to help them walk in snow. Some animals that live in the snow have special *adaptations* on their feet to help them. They don't need snowshoes! They are born with features that help them walk and survive in the snow.

Snow leopards live in the snow. These cats live high in the mountains of Central Asia. Their feet are covered with fur even on the bottom. The fur acts as natural snowshoes. They also have thick fur all over their bodies. The snow leopard uses its tail as a blanket, too. It can wrap its long tail around parts of its body that get cold.

The tail is also used to help snow leopards keep their balance on the steep mountain slopes. This helps them hunt in the mountains. Good balance helps snow leopards stay on their feet as they jump and chase prey. They have powerful legs and can jump very far, up to 50 feet. The snow leopards

Read · Reason · Write ·
© The Continental Press, Inc. **DUPLICATING THIS MATERIAL IS ILLEGAL.**

use this ability to help them catch their prey. They eat deer, boar, and blue sheep. Blue sheep are a type of sheep that live in the mountains in Central Asia. Snow leopards also eat rabbits and birds.

Sometimes snow leopards eat animals like goats and sheep. This makes people angry. Then the goat and sheep herders kill the cats. They want to keep their animals safe. Poachers also kill snow leopards. They sell the pelts even though it is against the law. *Pelt* is another name for the skin and fur of an animal. Some people like to wear the spotted fur. They use pelts to make hats and coats. Snow leopards are also used in traditional Chinese medicine.

Snow leopards are becoming extinct. People move into the cats' *habitats*. The leopards lose their homes. The people take up space. But they also kill other animals the snow leopard uses as food. People hunt blue sheep, rabbits, and birds for food. There are only about 6,000 snow leopards left in the world.

© The Continental Press, Inc.   DUPLICATING THIS MATERIAL IS ILLEGAL.

Understanding the Story

It is important to understand what you read. You just read a story about snow leopards. Did you read the story carefully? Here are some questions about the story. Read each one. Then fill in the circle beside the best answer. If you are not sure, go back and look at the story again.

1. How many snow leopards are left in the world?

Ⓐ 100

Ⓑ 600

Ⓒ 6,000

Ⓓ 50,000

Factual

2. How does people killing the snow leopards' prey affect the snow leopards?

Ⓐ Snow leopards are no longer hunted.

Ⓑ Snow leopards can't find food.

Ⓒ More snow leopards appear.

Ⓓ Farmers chase off the snow leopards.

Critical Reasoning

3. What helps snow leopards stay balanced while hunting?

Ⓐ their tails

Ⓑ their eyes

Ⓒ their ears

Ⓓ their claws

Factual

Read · Reason · Write ·

© The Continental Press, Inc.   **DUPLICATING THIS MATERIAL IS ILLEGAL.**

4. What *adaptations* help snow leopards walk in the snow?

Inference

  Ⓐ   fur on their feet

  Ⓑ   sharp claws

  Ⓒ   a long tail

  Ⓓ   thick fur

5. People use the snow leopards' pelts

Factual

  Ⓐ   to eat

  Ⓑ   for a pet

  Ⓒ   for shoes

  Ⓓ   for coats

6. A *habitat* is

Inference

  Ⓐ   something you do many times

  Ⓑ   a home

  Ⓒ   food

  Ⓓ   a newborn snow leopard

© The Continental Press, Inc.   **DUPLICATING THIS MATERIAL IS ILLEGAL.**

7. Snow leopards can be protected by

Critical Reasoning

  Ⓐ getting rid of their prey

  Ⓑ destroying their habitat

  Ⓒ allowing poachers to hunt

  Ⓓ creating a reserve for snow leopards

8. A snow leopard can jump up to

Factual

  Ⓐ 5 feet

  Ⓑ 25 feet

  Ⓒ 50 feet

  Ⓓ 500 feet

© The Continental Press, Inc. **DUPLICATING THIS MATERIAL IS ILLEGAL.**

Summing Up

You have learned some things about snow leopards. A **time line** is a special way to show a sequence of events. Look at the time line below and put the following events in order. The first one has been done for you.

There are fewer snow leopards.

People get angry.

Snow leopards eat domestic animals.

Snow leopards are killed.

Herders want to protect their animals.

Snow leopards eat domestic animals.

© The Continental Press, Inc. **DUPLICATING THIS MATERIAL IS ILLEGAL.**

Write About It

Writing can have many purposes. When you write a letter, you can tell people something you have learned. Write a letter to a friend and tell your friend what you have learned about snow leopards. Tell your friend what snow leopards eat, what special adaptations they have, and why they are endangered.

Dear _____,

Today I learned about snow leopards. Here are some interesting facts I learned. Snow leopards eat _____

_____

_____

_____

_____

Snow leopards live in the snow and they have special adaptations to help them survive. Some of their adaptations are _____

_____

_____

There are not many snow leopards left. They are endangered because

_____

_____

Hopefully, something can be done to help save these animals.

Sincerely yours,

_____

© The Continental Press, Inc. **DUPLICATING THIS MATERIAL IS ILLEGAL.**

Reviewing the Stories

Think about the stories you have read in Part I about endangered animals. What do you remember about Siberian tigers, African wild dogs, snow leopards, and Komodo dragons? Here are some questions about them. Read each one. Then fill in the circle beside the answer.

1. Siberian tigers, African wild dogs, snow leopards, and Komodo dragons all

   (A) live in the snow

   (B) live on land

   (C) lay eggs

   (D) live in Africa

   `Inference`

2. Which animals are predators?

   (A) snow leopards and blue sheep

   (B) African wild dogs and goats

   (C) Komodo dragons and deer

   (D) Siberian tigers and African wild dogs

   `Inference`

3. Which animal is a reptile?

   (A) the tiger

   (B) the snow leopard

   (C) the Komodo dragon

   (D) the African wild dog

   `Factual`

© The Continental Press, Inc.   **DUPLICATING THIS MATERIAL IS ILLEGAL.**

4. In the United States, where would you most likely see these animals?

Critical Reasoning

(A) in a pet store

(B) by a river

(C) in the forest

(D) at the zoo

5. All of these animals are

Inference

(A) friendly

(B) extinct

(C) endangered

(D) reptiles

6. If poachers kill many of the animals in these stories, the animals

Inference

(A) will move out of their habitats

(B) could become extinct

(C) will starve

(D) will become mean

© The Continental Press, Inc.   **DUPLICATING THIS MATERIAL IS ILLEGAL.**

7. Which of these animals would probably eat the most food?

Inference

Ⓐ a Siberian tiger

Ⓑ an African wild dog

Ⓒ a Komodo dragon

Ⓓ a snow leopard

8. Which of these animals might meet each other in their natural habitats?

Critical Reasoning

Ⓐ snow leopards and Siberian tigers

Ⓑ Siberian tigers and Komodo dragons

Ⓒ Komodo dragons and snow leopards

Ⓓ African wild dogs and Siberian tigers

© The Continental Press, Inc.   **DUPLICATING THIS MATERIAL IS ILLEGAL.**

Summing Up

Wild animals are not likely to be found in your backyard. The Siberian tiger, the African wild dog, the snow leopard, and the Komodo dragon are wild animals. They would not make good pets. Why not?

A **chart** is a good way to write down and sort your ideas. The chart below has been started for you. Fill in the rest of it. Tell why you think the animals you have read about would <u>not</u> make good pets.

Why They Are Not Good Pets

Siberian tiger	African wild dog	Komodo dragon	Snow leopard
eats too much	needs a pack of dogs	can be fierce	can be dangerous

© The Continental Press, Inc.   **DUPLICATING THIS MATERIAL IS ILLEGAL.**

Write About It

A **topic sentence** is the first sentence of a paragraph. It states the main idea of a paragraph. The other sentences in the paragraph tell something about the main idea. These sentences give facts, details, and examples.

An animal trainer at a zoo is giving a speech about why some animals would not make good pets. She is writing her speech first on paper. Help her complete her speech. The topic sentence is written for each paragraph. Write some sentences that tell about the main idea. Use the chart on page 36 to help you.

A Siberian tiger would not make a good pet.

_____

_____

_____

_____

_____

_____

An African wild dog would be just as bad as a pet.

_____

_____

_____

_____

_____

_____

© The Continental Press, Inc.   **DUPLICATING THIS MATERIAL IS ILLEGAL.**

A Komodo dragon would not make a good pet either.

_____

_____

_____

_____

_____

A snow leopard would not make a good pet.

_____

_____

_____

_____

_____

© The Continental Press, Inc.   **DUPLICATING THIS MATERIAL IS ILLEGAL.**

Meet the Monk Seal

The Hawaiians gave it a name that meant "dog that runs in rough waters." It looks a little like a dog, but it isn't. It's a Hawaiian monk seal, and it doesn't live anywhere but Hawaii. And it doesn't migrate either. Why would it want to leave Hawaii?

A monk seal weighs about 500 pounds and is 7 to 9 feet long. It likes to eat fish and lobsters. It can stay underwater for 15 to 20 minutes, and it doesn't need to come up for air because it can slow down its heartbeat. A slower heartbeat means it needs less air.

© The Continental Press, Inc.   **DUPLICATING THIS MATERIAL IS ILLEGAL.**

A mother monk seal has only one pup at a time. She gives the pup milk for about six weeks and, after that, the pup has to learn to fish. While the pup is nursing, the mother monk seal doesn't eat anything.

There are only about 1,000 monk seals left. It is the most endangered seal in United States waters. Every year, there are fewer monk seals. Sometimes they get caught in fishing nets. Sometimes fishermen catch too many lobsters, and the seals can't get enough to eat.

People used to hunt monk seals for their meat and skins. People don't hunt these animals anymore, but tiger sharks do. Most monk seals have scars left by these sharks, while a good many die from the attacks.

Monk seals stay by themselves. Each one likes to have its own private beach. There, it will lie in the sun and rest. Hawaiian monk seals are cute and friendly. They have always lived on islands with no people, so they never learned to be afraid. A monk seal won't run from you on the beach. It will just lie there. But never bother a monk seal. It needs its rest. If it goes back in the ocean when it is tired, a tiger shark could eat it!

© The Continental Press, Inc.   **DUPLICATING THIS MATERIAL IS ILLEGAL.**

Understanding the Story

It is important to understand what you read. You just read a story about monk seals. Did you read the story carefully? Here are some questions about the story. Read each one. Then fill in the circle beside the best answer. If you are not sure, go back and look at the story again.

1. The word *migrate* means to

   Ⓐ   catch lobsters

   Ⓑ   breathe underwater

   Ⓒ   swim away when you are afraid

   Ⓓ   move somewhere else in certain seasons

> **Critical Reasoning**

2. A mother monk seal will

   Ⓐ   nurse her baby and not eat anything herself

   Ⓑ   find fish for herself and her newborn pup

   Ⓒ   not be afraid of tiger sharks

   Ⓓ   not be able to swim

> **Inference**

3. How many monk seals are there?

   Ⓐ   about 100

   Ⓑ   about 1,000

   Ⓒ   about 5,000

   Ⓓ   about 10,000

> **Factual**

© The Continental Press, Inc. **DUPLICATING THIS MATERIAL IS ILLEGAL.**

4. To save the monk seal, people should

Inference

(A) make sure the seals don't get caught in fishing nets

(B) kill all the tiger sharks

(C) put the monk seals in zoos

(D) use their skins for coats

5. If you see a Hawaiian monk seal sleeping on the beach, you should

Inference

(A) keep it wet

(B) chase it back into the ocean

(C) stay away from it

(D) try to feed it

6. How much does a Hawaiian monk seal weigh?

Critical Reasoning

(A) more than an elephant

(B) less than a man

(C) as much as a big dog

(D) more than a big dog

© The Continental Press, Inc. **DUPLICATING THIS MATERIAL IS ILLEGAL.**

7. Why don't people hunt monk seals anymore?

Critical Reasoning

Ⓐ There are no monk seals left to hunt.

Ⓑ Hunters can see monk seals in zoos.

Ⓒ Hunters are afraid of the tiger sharks.

Ⓓ They no longer need the monk seals for meat and skins.

8. A Hawaiian monk seal can stay underwater for

Factual

Ⓐ 2 to 3 hours

Ⓑ 1 to 2 hours

Ⓒ 30 minutes to an hour

Ⓓ 15 to 20 minutes

© The Continental Press, Inc.   **DUPLICATING THIS MATERIAL IS ILLEGAL.**

Summing Up

This story gives you some information about Hawaiian monk seals. It told you some things that monk seals do.

A **chart** is a useful way to sort information. The chart below lists some animals and people form the story. Fill in the boxes. Write some action words that describe what these animals and people do.

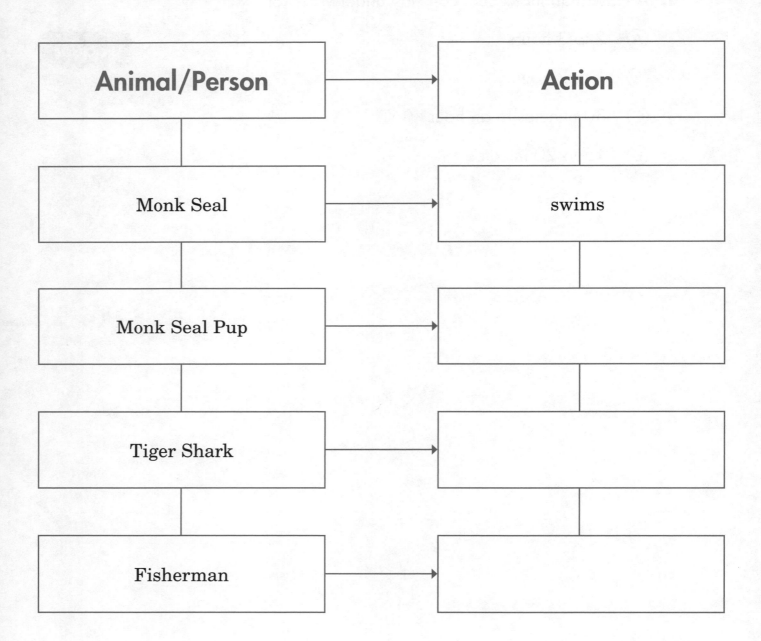

Animal/Person	→	Action
Monk Seal	→	swims
Monk Seal Pup	→	
Tiger Shark	→	
Fisherman	→	

Read · Reason · Write · · · · · · · · · · · · ·

© The Continental Press, Inc.   **DUPLICATING THIS MATERIAL IS ILLEGAL.**

Write About It

A **sentence** tells a complete idea. It has two parts. One part tells what the sentence is about. This is the **subject.** The subject is usually a noun. The other part of the sentence is the **predicate.** This is usually a verb.

Write your own complete sentences. For each number below, there is a subject and a predicate. Put the words together to make a sentence. You can add extra words to make your sentences more exciting. Use your chart to help you.

1.   monk seal   swims

<u>The monk seal swims in the ocean.</u>

2.   tiger shark   eats

_____

3.   fishermen   catch

_____

4.   pups   play

_____

5.   mothers   feed

_____

6.   people   see

_____

© The Continental Press, Inc.   **DUPLICATING THIS MATERIAL IS ILLEGAL.**

This story is about turtles that live in the ocean. Read the story. Then answer the questions that follow.

Green Sea Turtles

It is night. A mother green sea turtle crawls from the ocean and slowly makes her way up on the beach. It is hard work. Her flippers are good for swimming, but not for pulling her large weight across the sand. Finally, she makes it and starts to dig a hole. In the hole, she buries 100 eggs. Then she covers the hole with sand. She is exhausted, but she crawls slowly back to the ocean.

In about two months, baby sea turtles hatch from the eggs. They start to dig out of the sand, but the sand feels hot. They wait. When the sand feels cool, they know it is night. Then they dig out and rush for the ocean, but some don't make it. Crabs or birds eat them. When they finally reach the ocean, fish eat many more of them. Very few grow up to be big green sea turtles.

Green sea turtles are reptiles. They can weigh up to 500 pounds and can live to be 60 years old. They live in the ocean, but they have to breathe air as people do. Usually the

© The Continental Press, Inc.   **DUPLICATING THIS MATERIAL IS ILLEGAL.**

turtles come up for air every few minutes. But when they are sleeping, they can stay underwater for more than 2 hours!

These creatures are different from turtles that live on land. Their shells are lighter, so they can float. They cannot pull their heads into their shells for protection. Instead of legs, they have flippers for swimming. They can also swim hundreds of miles and can go as fast as 35 miles an hour.

The green sea turtle's shell is mostly brown. The animal eats plants, so its body fat is greenish. Also, its shell has green algae on it, so it looks green. Fish eat the algae from the turtle's shell. The fish get an easy meal, and the turtle gets a clean shell. When two animals help each other like this, it is called *symbiosis*.

The green sea turtle has only two known predators—sharks and people. Sharks like to eat these tasty turtles, and so do people. People also dig up the eggs for food and make jewelry and other things from the turtle's shell. The beaches where turtles lay their eggs are also changing. People build hotels and homes on the beaches. The sea turtles have no place to lay their eggs.

At one time there were millions of green sea turtles in oceans all over the world. Today, there are fewer than 200,000. These turtles have existed since dinosaurs roamed Earth 150 million years ago. Let's hope they don't ever die out.

© The Continental Press, Inc.   **DUPLICATING THIS MATERIAL IS ILLEGAL.**

Understanding the Story

Here are some questions about the story that you just read. Read each one. Then fill in the circle beside the best answer. If you are not sure, go back and look at the story again.

1. This story tells about

   Ⓐ an animal that breathes underwater with gills

   Ⓑ an animal that lives in the ocean and breathes air

   Ⓒ the biggest animal in the ocean

   Ⓓ the smallest animal in the ocean

   Inference

2. Which is <u>true</u> about the green sea turtle?

   Ⓐ The green sea turtle cannot swim very far.

   Ⓑ The green sea turtle can run very fast on land.

   Ⓒ The green sea turtle has a green shell.

   Ⓓ The green sea turtle is a reptile and lays eggs.

   Inference

3. One green sea turtle probably lays so many eggs because

   Ⓐ not many baby turtles ever grow up

   Ⓑ people like to eat the eggs

   Ⓒ it is a very big animal

   Ⓓ not many of the eggs will hatch

   Critical Reasoning

© The Continental Press, Inc.   **DUPLICATING THIS MATERIAL IS ILLEGAL.**

4. How are sea turtles different from land turtles?

Ⓐ   Sea turtles have flippers and their shells are lighter.

Ⓑ   Sea turtles are always bigger than land turtles.

Ⓒ   Sea turtles can run faster than land turtles.

Ⓓ   Sea turtles never go on land, and land turtles never go in the water.

5. *Symbiosis* means that

Ⓐ   plants can grow on the green sea turtle's shell

Ⓑ   fish like to eat algae

Ⓒ   two different animals are alike

Ⓓ   two different animals help each other

6. To save the green sea turtle, which of these is the best thing for people to do?

Ⓐ   wear jewelry made from a green sea turtle's shell

Ⓑ   eat the green sea turtle's eggs

Ⓒ   help protect the habitats of the green sea turtle

Ⓓ   eat soup made from green sea turtles

© The Continental Press, Inc.   **DUPLICATING THIS MATERIAL IS ILLEGAL.**

7. A *predator* is

Inference

Ⓐ an animal that is usually eaten by another animal

Ⓑ always a shark

Ⓒ an animal that kills other animals for food

Ⓓ never found in the ocean

8. Algae is probably most like

Critical Reasoning

Ⓐ sharks

Ⓑ turtle eggs

Ⓒ a clean turtle shell

Ⓓ seaweed

© The Continental Press, Inc. **DUPLICATING THIS MATERIAL IS ILLEGAL.**

Summing Up

You know some things about green sea turtles. You know what they look like, things they do, and why they are endangered.

An **informational map** is a good way to record things you have learned. Fill in the map below. Write down some things you've learned about the green sea turtle.

The Green Sea Turtle

What It Looks Like

Things It Does

Why It Is Endangered

© The Continental Press, Inc.   **DUPLICATING THIS MATERIAL IS ILLEGAL.**

Write About It

Good writers make notes before they write. Good notes help a writer organize a story. The notes give writers ideas. When you have good notes, it is easier to write good sentences and paragraphs. Suppose you went swimming in the ocean and saw a green sea turtle. What would you say about it? Write a letter to a friend to tell about the green sea turtle. Look at the story for ideas. You can use the information you wrote in the chart on page 51, too.

Dear _____ ,

Today I went swimming in the ocean. I saw a green sea turtle! It looked

like _____

_____

_____

The green sea turtle swam right past me! It was _____

_____

_____

_____

I found out that the green sea turtle is endangered. It is endangered

because _____

_____

_____

Your friend,

_____

© The Continental Press, Inc.   DUPLICATING THIS MATERIAL IS ILLEGAL.

The Giant Clam

A giant clam doesn't do much. It doesn't move around, and it doesn't hunt for food. It doesn't even make much noise. But it's enormous! The giant clam can weigh almost 500 pounds and grow to be over 4 feet long. That is really big for a clam.

A giant clam is very beautiful. It has two huge shells called *valves*. Inside the valves is a colorful blue, green, and yellow *mantle*. This mantle is the fleshy part of the clam. You can see the mantle if you go diving because the clam usually sits on the ocean floor with its two valves wide open.

Giant clams live on reefs in shallow water. There isn't much food there so the giant clam has adaptations to help it survive. It has its own food supply called *algae*. Algae live inside the clam, which uses them as food. The algae need sunlight to live. That's why the clam sits with its valves

© The Continental Press, Inc.   DUPLICATING THIS MATERIAL IS ILLEGAL.

open—to let sunlight in for the algae. In this way, the clam feeds the algae, and the algae feed the clam. As you know from reading about the green sea turtle, this is called *symbiosis*.

Giant clams are neither male or female. They are both, and one clam can make many baby clams. These tiny clams swim around for about a week but fish or crabs will eat many of them. After a week, the little clams find a place to settle down and grow. They grow very fast, and they get a very thick shell. Once a giant clam is big, only an octopus is strong enough to open it.

Giant clams are endangered. People eat too many of them and they also use the shells to make beautiful objects, like bowls and even tiles for floors. People also like to put giant clams in their fish tanks. Many baby clams are caught and sold for aquariums.

But people also help these quiet giants. The clams are easy to raise in clam nurseries. After all, they don't need food. They just need good water and the right amount of sun. When the clams are big enough, they are put back in the ocean. There, they will sit quietly and make more giant clams.

© The Continental Press, Inc.   **DUPLICATING THIS MATERIAL IS ILLEGAL.**

Understanding the Story

Here are some questions about the story that you just read. Read each one. Then fill in the circle beside the best answer. If you are not sure, go back and look at the story again.

1. This story is mainly about

    Ⓐ food we get from the ocean

    Ⓑ the biggest clam in the world

    Ⓒ quiet sea monsters

    Ⓓ algae and the clam

Inference

2. A clam's *mantle* is

    Ⓐ the fleshy part

    Ⓑ its shell

    Ⓒ the algae

    Ⓓ its mouth

Factual

3. Giant clams live best in shallow water because

    Ⓐ there are lots of octopuses

    Ⓑ people can see them

    Ⓒ sunlight can reach them

    Ⓓ they move to the surface to breathe

Critical Reasoning

© The Continental Press, Inc. **DUPLICATING THIS MATERIAL IS ILLEGAL.**

4. The only predators that can eat full-grown giant clams are

(A) other giant clams

(B) people and octopuses

(C) sharks and lobsters

(D) algae

Inference

5. When an animal *adapts,* it

(A) learns to eat algae instead of other foods

(B) creates a mantle to protect itself

(C) changes in order to live in its habitat

(D) makes food out of sunlight

Factual

6. People help clams by

(A) eating them

(B) making things out of their shells

(C) killing the octopus

(D) raising them in nurseries

Inference

© The Continental Press, Inc.   **DUPLICATING THIS MATERIAL IS ILLEGAL.**

7. Which living thing helps the giant clam?

Factual

Ⓐ the octopus

Ⓑ algae

Ⓒ the crab

Ⓓ fish

8. Why might a baby clam not live very long?

Inference

Ⓐ It gets tired from swimming around.

Ⓑ Its shell is too heavy.

Ⓒ It gets eaten by fish and crabs.

Ⓓ It doesn't have any algae yet.

© The Continental Press, Inc. **DUPLICATING THIS MATERIAL IS ILLEGAL.**

Summing Up

This story gave you some information about the giant clam. You can use what you have learned about the giant clam to write a story.

An **information chart** is a way to help you sort ideas in a clear way. In the chart below, the words above the boxes tell you what information to write about. Fill in the chart with information about the giant clam.

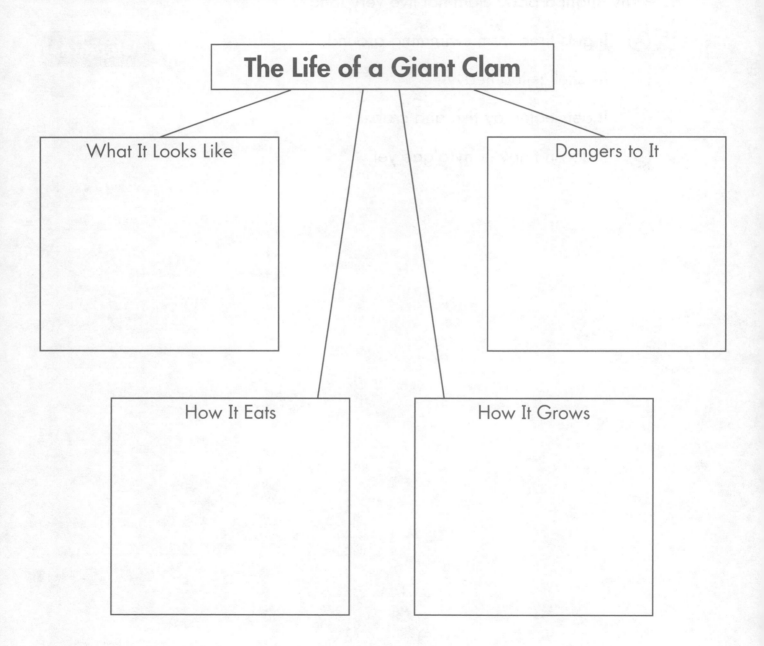

The Life of a Giant Clam

What It Looks Like

Dangers to It

How It Eats

How It Grows

© The Continental Press, Inc.   **DUPLICATING THIS MATERIAL IS ILLEGAL.**

Write About It

Some signs give us information. Some signs tell us things we need to know. People who write signs must be able to write the information so people can understand it.

If you visited a clam nursery, you would probably read signs about clams. Help the nursery workers complete the signs for the nursery. Use the notes you made on the chart on page 58 to write the signs.

What a Giant Clam Eats
A giant clam does not need to look for food. This is how a giant clam eats.

_____

_____

_____

_____

How a Giant Clam Grows
A giant clam starts off as a small baby clam. For the first week, it _____

_____

_____

_____

_____

Dangers to the Giant Clam
Only two things are really harmful to the giant clam. They are _____

_____

_____

_____

_____

© The Continental Press, Inc. **DUPLICATING THIS MATERIAL IS ILLEGAL.**

This story is about one of the world's most important predators. Read the story. Then answer the questions that follow.

"Jagged Tooth"

The great white shark is at the *apex* of the food chain, which means it is the top predator in the ocean. Great white sharks hunt seals, rays, bony fish, squids, dolphins, and whales. They even eat other sharks. Their only rival is the killer whale. The killer whale is at the top of the food chain, too. Killer whales have been known to eat great white sharks. But this doesn't happen very often.

Its scientific name is *Carcharodon carcharias*. This means "jagged tooth."

A great white shark's mouth is full of rows of teeth. Its upper jaw holds 26 teeth in each row. These teeth are used for cutting and sawing. The bottom jaw has 24 teeth in each row used for impaling. Great white sharks lose these teeth regularly but luckily they grow back throughout their life.

These sharks don't know if something is edible or not until they taste it. They have special organs in their mouths that help them decide if prey is edible or not. If the shark bites something inedible, it spits it out.

© The Continental Press, Inc.   **DUPLICATING THIS MATERIAL IS ILLEGAL.**

Sharks also use their sense of sight and smell. They can smell extremely well. They can detect faint traces of chemicals in the water. This helps them hunt and interact with other great white sharks. The pores on their snouts have a special jelly that aids prey detection. It also helps the sharks tell where they are going.

Great white sharks can see about as well as you. But they have a special eyelid that lets them roll their eyes back in their sockets to protect their eyes when eating. They also have built-in "glasses" and can see in low light.

Great white sharks can grow to be very big. They can grow up to 21 feet in length. The largest great white sharks can weigh 4,400 pounds. They are the world's largest predatory fish. Because of the sharks' teeth and big bodies, people are very scared of great white sharks.

These underwater creatures are endangered. One reason that they are hunted is that people like to eat their fins. Fishermen kill the sharks just for their fins. People also kill sharks because the huge animals frighten them. But great whites are very important to our oceans. They are the top predators and help maintain the ecosystem.

© The Continental Press, Inc.   DUPLICATING THIS MATERIAL IS ILLEGAL.

Understanding the Story

Here are some questions about the story that you just read. Read each one. Then fill in the circle beside the best answer. If you are not sure, go back and look at the story again.

1. This story tells about

   Ⓐ a dangerous animal that should be killed

   Ⓑ a predator that lives in the ocean

   Ⓒ the biggest animal in the ocean

   Ⓓ the smallest animal in the ocean

   Inference

2. Which is <u>true</u> about the great white shark?

   Ⓐ Its teeth won't grow back if lost.

   Ⓑ It doesn't have any rivals.

   Ⓒ It cannot smell well.

   Ⓓ It is the largest fish that hunts.

   Inference

3. Great white sharks have all these special eye adaptations <u>except</u> they can't

   Ⓐ see in the dark

   Ⓑ roll their eyes back into their sockets

   Ⓒ use special built-in glasses

   Ⓓ see in low light

   Inference

© The Continental Press, Inc. **DUPLICATING THIS MATERIAL IS ILLEGAL.**

4. Being at the *apex* of the food chain means great white sharks

Critical Reasoning

  (A) don't have any prey

  (B) eat everything

  (C) have very few predators

  (D) are the largest animal in the ocean

5. How does the great white shark's sense of smell help it?

Factual

  (A) It helps it sense danger.

  (B) Its sense of smell doesn't help.

  (C) A great white shark can't smell.

  (D) It helps a great white shark hunt.

6. The great white shark is called *jagged tooth* because

Inference

  (A) it has lots of sharp teeth

  (B) it loses its teeth

  (C) its teeth tear easily

  (D) it has one rough tooth

© The Continental Press, Inc. **DUPLICATING THIS MATERIAL IS ILLEGAL.**

7. Why are the great white sharks rivals of killer whales?

(A) Great white sharks eat killer whales.

(B) Killer whales eat great white sharks.

(C) They are both dangerous.

(D) They eat the same prey.

Critical Reasoning

8. People can protect sharks by

(A) making a shark reserve in the ocean

(B) killing their predators

(C) making it illegal to hunt sharks

(D) capturing them

Critical Reasoning

© The Continental Press, Inc.   **DUPLICATING THIS MATERIAL IS ILLEGAL.**

Summing Up

You know some things about great white sharks. You know what they look like, things they do, and why they are endangered.

An **information map** is a good way to sort information about what you have learned. Fill in the map below. Write down some things you've learned about the great white shark.

The Great White Shark

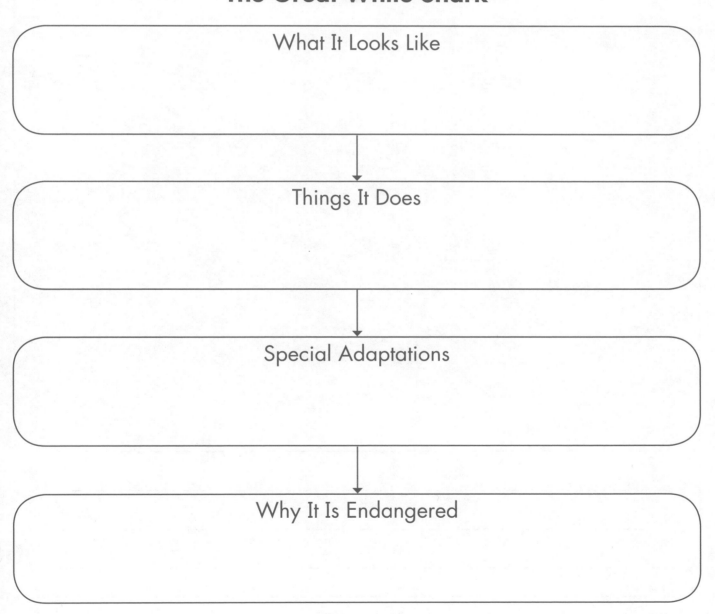

What It Looks Like

↓

Things It Does

↓

Special Adaptations

↓

Why It Is Endangered

© The Continental Press, Inc.   **DUPLICATING THIS MATERIAL IS ILLEGAL.**

Write About It

A **caption** is words that tell about a picture. The caption comes right under the picture. Draw a picture of a great white shark and write a caption for the picture you drew.

© The Continental Press, Inc.   **DUPLICATING THIS MATERIAL IS ILLEGAL.**

Reviewing the Stories

Think about the stories you have read in Part II about endangered species. What do you remember about the Hawaiian monk seal, the green sea turtle, the giant clam, and the great white shark? Here are some questions about them. Read each one. Then fill in the circle beside the answer. If you are not sure, go back to the stories and look at them again.

1. How are Hawaiian monk seals, green sea turtles, giant clams, and great white sharks alike?

   Ⓐ They all breathe air.

   Ⓑ They all live in the ocean.

   Ⓒ They all lay eggs.

   Ⓓ They are all reptiles.

   Inference

2. Which is true about Hawaiian monk seals, green sea turtles, giant clams, and great white sharks?

   Ⓐ They are all good swimmers.

   Ⓑ Two of them are extinct.

   Ⓒ They all eat algae.

   Ⓓ They are all endangered animals.

   Inference

3. Which of these animals is a predator?

   Ⓐ Hawaiian monk seal

   Ⓑ green sea turtle

   Ⓒ algae

   Ⓓ giant clam

   Critical Reasoning

© The Continental Press, Inc. **DUPLICATING THIS MATERIAL IS ILLEGAL.**

4. Which of these animals is a reptile?

Factual

   Ⓐ Hawaiian monk seal

   Ⓑ green sea turtle

   Ⓒ great white shark

   Ⓓ giant clam

5. Which animal is probably the most playful in the water?

   Ⓐ Hawaiian monk seal

   Ⓑ green sea turtle

Critical Reasoning

   Ⓒ great white shark

   Ⓓ giant clam

6. Which two animals both breathe air?

   Ⓐ Hawaiian monk seal and great white shark

   Ⓑ green sea turtle and giant clam

Inference

   Ⓒ giant clam and Hawaiian monk seal

   Ⓓ Hawaiian monk seal and green sea turtle

© The Continental Press, Inc. **DUPLICATING THIS MATERIAL IS ILLEGAL.**

7. Which creature is a predator of Hawaiian monk seals, green sea turtles, and giant clams?

Ⓐ tiger shark

Ⓑ octopus

Ⓒ people

Ⓓ algae

8. The word *symbiosis* is part of the lives of which two animals?

Inference

Ⓐ Hawaiian monk seal and tiger shark

Ⓑ giant clam and Hawaiian monk seal

Ⓒ green sea turtle and giant clam

Ⓓ octopus and giant clam

© The Continental Press, Inc.   DUPLICATING THIS MATERIAL IS ILLEGAL.

Summing Up

Endangered animals are harmed by people. But people try to help endangered animals, too. One way to look at how things are alike and how they are different is to write about them in a **comparison chart.** Fill in the chart below to tell about the endangered animals you read about.

	Hawaiian Monk Seal	Green Sea Turtle	Giant Clam	Great White Shark
How People Harm Them				
How People Help Them				

© The Continental Press, Inc.   **DUPLICATING THIS MATERIAL IS ILLEGAL.**

Write About It

Writing can have many purposes. Sometimes writers write to tell their **opinions** about something. The writers try to persuade others to feel the same way. To do that, they have to back up their opinions with **facts.** These facts help their arguments.

People sometimes write to a newspaper to state their opinions. This is called an **editorial.** An editorial about endangered animals has been started below. Read the first few sentences. Complete the editorial by writing about what you learned. Use information you wrote in your chart on page 70, too.

The Hawaiian monk seal, the green sea turtle, the giant clam, and the great white shark are endangered animals. Their worst enemy is people.

_____

_____

_____

_____

_____

_____

_____

_____

_____

_____

_____

© The Continental Press, Inc.   **DUPLICATING THIS MATERIAL IS ILLEGAL.**

We can help these animals from becoming extinct. For example, we can

_____

_____

_____

_____

_____

_____

_____

_____

_____

_____

© The Continental Press, Inc. **DUPLICATING THIS MATERIAL IS ILLEGAL.**